Colorful Projects for Outdoor Fun

COMPILED BY **Barbara Delaney**

INTERWEAVE
interweave.com

Contents

The projects in this collection were originally published in other Interweave publications, including 101 Patchwork, Modern Patchwork, Quilt Scene, Quilting Arts, *and* Stitch *magazines. Some have been altered to update information and/or conform to space limitations.*

Interweave
A division of F+W Media, Inc.
201 East Fourth Street
Loveland, CO 80537
interweave.com

Manufactured in the United States by Versa Press

ISBN 978-1-62033-561-1 (pbk.)

4   **Sunset Picnic Ensemble**
Carol Zentgraf

7   **Handy Gardener's Apron**
Sarah Minshall

10   **Roll-Up Outdoor Concert Quilt**
Lisa Chin

13   **Liberty & Linen Spring Hat**
Melissa Frantz

16   **Water Bottle Carrier**
Diane Rusin Doran

19 So Simple Head Wrap
Ellen Seeburger

21 Roll-Up Reversible
Stadium Blanket
Carol Zentgraf

23 Patchwork Lunch Sack
Sarah Minshall

26 Convertible Beach Towel-Bag
Ali Winston

29 Quilt Sling
Marijka Walker

30 Lazy Days Hammock
Carol Zentgraf

33 Hexagon Beach Bag
Ayumi Takahashi

38 Playful Beach Bucket
Linda Turner Griepentrog

40 Essential Sunglasses Case
Debbie Grifka

42 Sewing Basics

Sunset Picnic Ensemble

BY CAROL ZENTGRAF

Celebrate summer eves with this colorful beach blanket and coordinating beverage or lunch tote. The blanket features a layer of batting for comfort and a laminated backing for protection from damp sand—perfect for a wonderful beach dinner spent watching the sunset. The roomy tote with removable divider will hold two beverage bottles or a hearty lunch. The insulated lining of the bag helps maintain the temperature of chilled or warm contents.

Picnic Blanket

Materials

- □ 1⅛ yd (103 cm) of cotton print for center panel
- □ 1⅔ yd (152.5 cm) of coordinating cotton print for borders
- □ 1⅔ yd (152.5 cm) of laminated cotton print for backing
- □ 56" × 60" (142 × 152.5 cm) piece of low-loft batting

Finished Size

56" × 60" (142 × 152.5 cm)

Notes

* All seam allowances are ½" (1.3 cm).

* Sew seams with right sides together.

* Use a press cloth when pressing laminated fabrics. Do not touch the iron directly to the fabric.

Insulated Tote

Materials

- □ 1 yd (91.5 cm) of cotton print for outside of tote and strap
- □ ¾ yd (68.5 cm) of coordinating laminated cotton print for lining
- □ 1 yd (91.5 cm) of cotton print to match laminated fabric for divider and binding
- □ ¾ yd (68.5 cm) of insulated batting, such as Insul-Bright
- □ One 5½" × 9½" (14 × 24 cm) rectangle and two 8" × 12" (20.5 × 30.5 cm) rectangles of heavyweight, double-sided fusible interfacing
- □ 7" (18 cm) length of ¾" (2 cm) hook-and-loop tape
- □ 3 yd (274.5 cm) of ¼" (6 mm) double-stick fusible web tape
- □ Temporary spray adhesive
- □ ½" (1.3 cm) bias tape maker (optional)

Finished Size

13" × 8½" × 4½" (33 × 21.5 × 11.5 cm)

Notes

* All seam allowances are ½" (1.3 cm).

* Sew seams with right sides together.

* Use a press cloth when pressing laminated fabrics. Do not touch the iron directly to the fabric.

Picnic Blanket

CUT THE FABRIC

1 For the center panel, cut one 42" × 45" (106.5 × 114.5 cm) rectangle.

2 For the borders, cut two 8" × 42" (20.5 × 106.5 cm) strips for the ends and two 8" × 60" (20.5 × 152.5 cm) strips for the sides.

3 For the backing, cut one 56" × 60" (142 × 152.5 cm) rectangle.

PIECE THE TOP

4 Sew the two end border strips to the two 42" (106.5 cm) edges of the center panel. Press the seam allowances toward the borders.

5 Sew the two long border strips to the top and bottom edges. Press the seam allowances toward the borders.

ASSEMBLE THE BLANKET

6 Place the backing right-side up on a large flat surface. Place the pieced top right-side down on the backing and the batting on the wrong side of the pieced top. Pin the layers together. Sew the layers together, leaving an 18" (45.5 cm) opening in the center of one edge for turning.

7 Turn right-side out and press, pressing the opening seam allowances under.

8 Slip-stitch the opening closed.

9 Topstitch around the entire blanket ⅜" (1 cm) from the edge.

Insulated Tote

CUT THE FABRIC

10 From the cotton print fabric for the outside of the tote, cut one 9½" × 14½" (24 × 37 cm) rectangle for the front, one 9½" × 19½" (24 × 49.5 cm) rectangle for the back, two 5½" × 14½" (14 × 37 cm) rectangles for the sides, one 5½" × 9½" (14 × 24 cm) rectangle for the bottom, and one 2½" × 38" (6.5 × 96.5 cm) strip for the strap.

11 From the laminated fabric, cut one 9½" × 14½" (24 × 37 cm) rectangle for the front, one 9½" × 19½" (24 × 49.5 cm) rectangle for the back, and two 5½" × 14½" (14 × 37 cm) rectangles for the sides, and one 5½" × 9½" (14 × 24 cm) rectangle for the bottom.

12 From the remaining cotton print fabric, cut four 8" × 12" (20.5 × 30.5 cm) rectangles for the divider and one 2½" × 38" (6.5 × 96.5 cm) strip for the strap. For the binding, cut and piece 2" (5 cm) wide bias strips to measure 115" (292 cm).

13 From the insulated batting, cut one 9½" × 14½" (24 × 37 cm) rectangle for the front, one 9½" × 19½" (24 × 49.5 cm) rectangle for the back, two 5½" × 14½" (14 × 37 cm) rectangles for the sides, and one 5½" × 9½" (14 × 24 cm) rectangle for the bottom.

ASSEMBLE THE TOTE

14 For the bottom of the tote, fuse the heavyweight interfacing bottom rectangle to the wrong side of the outside fabric bottom rectangle and the bottom batting rectangle.

15 Spray the wrong sides of the tote outside fabric rectangles with spray adhesive. Adhere a matching batting rectangle to the wrong side of each fabric rectangle.

16 To assemble the outside of the tote, sew the side panels to the front and back panels with the bottom edges even and beginning ½" (1.3 cm) from the bottom edge. Sew the bottom panel in place. Repeat to sew the lining pieces together.

17 Turn the outside of the tote right-side out and press. Insert the lining with wrong sides together, edges even, and side seams aligned. Stitch the edges together ¼" (6 mm) from the edge.

18 To make the bias binding, sew the short ends of the bias strips together. Use a bias tape maker to make ½" (1.3 cm) wide double-fold bias binding. Or, press the strip in half lengthwise with wrong sides together. Open the strip and press the long edges under to meet at the center crease. Press in half lengthwise again.

19 For ease in even application, apply fusible web tape to the wrong side of both long bias binding edges. Remove the paper backing as you apply the tape. Beginning at one corner of the top flap, wrap the binding over the edges of the tote top and flap. Measure to make sure it is ½" (1.3 cm) wide on each side and fuse in place. Stitch ⅛" (3 mm) from the edge of the binding.

20 To make the strap, sew the long edges of the handle strips together. Press in half with wrong sides together along the seam line. Open the strip and press the long edges under to the center seam. Press in half again and stitch ⅛" (3 mm) from both long edges, stitching the open edges together. Turn the ends under 1" (2.5 cm) and stitch in place. Center each end of the strap on a side panel of the tote with the handle end 3" (7.5 cm) from the tote edge. Stitch the handle ends in place just below the binding. Stitch back and forth across the top and bottom of the handle stitching for extra stability.

21 Sew all edges of the hook strip of the hook-and-loop tape to the inside of the flap, aligning the top edge with the binding. Fold the flap to the front of the tote and mark the placement for the loop strip of the tape. Sew in place around all edges.

MAKE DIVIDER

22 Fuse the fabric rectangles to each side of the heavyweight interfacing.

23 Refer to Step 10 and stitch bias binding around each fabric-covered rectangle.

24 With the rectangles positioned horizontally, use a ruler and disappearing fabric marker to draw vertical lines dividing each rectangle in thirds. Fold the rectangles along the marked lines.

25 Align the folded rectangles with the center sections back to back and the ends folded outward. Stitch the center sections together along the top and bottom edges. Place the insert in the tote bag with the center section running from the front to the back.

Some materials for this project were supplied by Fairfield, C&T, Sulky, Warm Company, and Westminster Fabrics. ✍

CAROL ZENTGRAF is a writer, designer, and editor, specializing in sewing, embroidery, textiles, painting, and decorating. She designs for several magazines and fabric company websites. Carol is the author of seven home decor sewing books.

Laminated fabrics and cotton combine to make a dynamic picnic duo.

A handy insert keeps fragile contents intact.

Handy Gardener's Apron

BY SARAH MINSHALL

Keep your gardening tools close at hand while keeping your clothes tidy. Sturdy denim makes this apron perfect for outdoor use and ample pockets will hold a variety of garden implements.

Materials

☐ ¾ yd (68.5 cm) of lightweight denim, lightweight canvas, or heavyweight muslin for Pocket Fronts and Apron Body

☐ 5 coordinated print cottons, each piece about 9" × 3" (23 × 7.5 cm) for Pocket Tops

☐ ¼ yd (23 cm) solid color cotton for Pocket Backings

☐ ⅓ yd (30.5 cm) coordinating quilting cotton for Apron Backing

☐ ½ yd (45.5 cm) lightweight fusible interfacing

☐ Coordinating machine sewing thread

☐ Handsewing needle

☐ Scissors

☐ Straight pins

☐ Ruler

☐ Rotary cutter, rigid acrylic ruler, and self-healing mat (optional)

Finished Size

18" wide × 10½" tall (45.5 × 26.5 cm) without ties

Notes

* Seam allowances are ½" (1.3 cm) unless otherwise noted.

* Refer to **FIGURE 1** for pocket placement instructions.

Cut the Fabric

1 From the denim, cut:

— One each of the following Pocket Fronts:

Pocket 1: 6" × 3½" (15 × 9 cm)

Pocket 2: 6" × 7½" (15 × 19 cm)

Pocket 3: 6½" × 7½" (16.5 × 19 cm)

Pocket 4: 8½" × 3½" (21.5 × 9 cm)

Pocket 5: 8½" × 7½" (21.5 × 19 cm)

— Two Apron Ties, each 42" × 3" (106.5 × 7.5 cm)

— One Apron Body, 19" × 11½" (48.5 × 29 cm)

2 From the five coordinated print cottons, cut the following Pocket Tops:

— Pocket 1: cut 2, 6" × 3" (15 × 7.5 cm)

— Pocket 2: cut 2, 6" × 3" (15 × 7.5 cm)

— Pocket 3: cut 1, 6½" × 3" (16.5 × 7.5 cm)

— Pocket 4: cut 2, 8½" × 3" (21.5 × 7.5 cm)

— Pocket 5: cut 2, 8½" × 3" (21.5 × 7.5 cm)

3 Cut the solid cotton Pocket Backings as follows:

— Pocket 1: 6" long × 6" tall (15 × 15 cm)

— Pocket 2: 6" long × 10" tall (15 × 25.5 cm)

— Pocket 3: 6½" long × 10" tall (16.5 × 25.5 cm)

— Pocket 4: 8½" long × 6" tall (21.5 × 15 cm)

— Pocket 5: 8½" long × 10" tall (15 × 25.5 cm)

4 From the coordinating quilting cotton, cut a 19" × 11½" (48.5 × 29 cm) rectangle for the Apron Backing.

5 From the fusible interfacing, cut one piece 19" × 11½" (48.5 × 29 cm).

Sew the Pocket Pieces

6 For each pocket, pin the denim Pocket Front to the quilting cotton Pocket Top, right sides facing, along the long side.

7 Using a ¼" (6 mm) seam allowance, sew along the edge.

8 Press all seams to one side. The top of the pocket is now the printed cotton with a denim bottom.

9 Match each printed pocket unit with its matching solid cotton lining, pinning right sides together along the long side.

10 Using a ¼" (6 mm) seam allowance, sew along the long top edge.

11 Press all seams to one side.

Assemble the Pockets Together

12 Fold Pockets 1 and 4 so that the lining is lying flat on the back of the pocket, showing only the printed cotton/denim pocket unit.

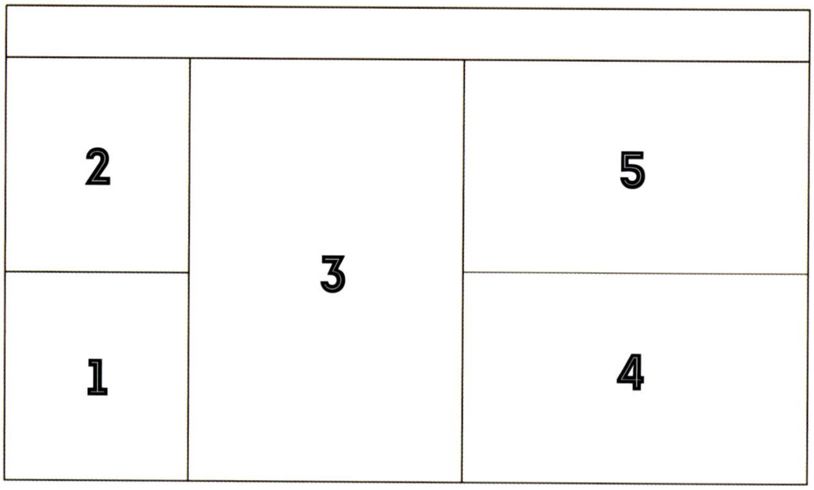

figure 1

13 Open Pocket 2 fully, so that the lining is completely exposed.

14 Pin Pocket 1, with right-side up, to Pocket 2 with its right-side up and lining fully out. Match the bottom and right edge together.

15 With Pockets 1 and 2 still just pinned together, fully open Pocket 3.

16 Pin the left edge of Pocket 3, with right sides facing, to the right edge of Pockets 1 and 2. You will be pinning the right sides of the lining together too.

17 Using a ¼" (6 mm) seam allowance, sew the two pocket-panels together.

18 Press seams open.

19 Repeat Steps 12–13, replacing Pockets 1 and 2 with Pockets 4 and 5.

20 Pin Pocket 4 with right-side up to Pocket 5 with right-side up and lining fully out. Match the bottom and left edge together.

21 Pin the right edge of Pocket 3 (now connected to Pockets 1 and 2) to the left edge of Pockets 4 and 5. You will be pinning the right sides of the lining together too.

22 Sew all three pockets together.

23 Press seams open.

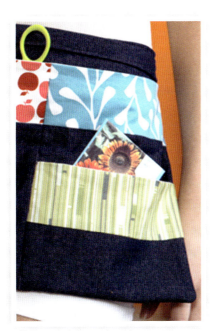

Efficient multilayered pockets create lots of room in this neat apron.

24 Fold solid cotton lining over so that the quilting cotton is now at the top of the pocket set. Press seam flat.

Attach Pockets to Denim Panel

25 Following the manufacturer's instructions, iron the fusible interfacing to the wrong side of the denim.

26 With the right side of the denim facing up, place the pockets right-side up on top. Match the bottom and sides.

27 Pin along the sides of the piece, making sure that the pockets are completely straight and flat.

28 Using a ¼" (6 mm) seam, baste the pockets to the edge of the denim panel along the right and left sides.

29 To create pockets, sew down the seam line between Pockets 1, 2, and 3. Backstitch at the top and bottom to secure.

30 Repeat Step 29 to sew along the seam between Pockets 3, 4, and 5.

Make the Apron Ties

31 Fold one of the 42" × 3" (106.5 × 7.5 cm) denim pieces in half lengthwise and press.

32 Fold one long edge into the newly pressed center and press.

33 Fold the remaining edge into the center and press.

34 Pin along the open edge.

35 Using an ⅛" (3 mm) seam allowance, sew along both edges of the tie.

36 Tie a knot at one end of the tie, with the raw edges still exposed.

37 Repeat Steps 31–36 for the second tie.

Sew the Apron Together

38 Place the cotton backing (which measures 19" × 11½" [48.5 × 29 cm]) and the denim panel and pockets unit right sides together. Pin along the top edge.

39 Backstitch to secure, and sew along the top edge of the apron.

40 On the right side of the apron, pin the end of the apron tie without the knot right below the top seam. Match the edge of the tie with the edge of the apron.

41 Pin and sew along the right side.

42 Repeat Steps 40–41 for the left side.

43 Tuck the apron ties inside, and pin along the bottom of the apron.

44 Sew along the bottom, leaving a 4" (10 cm) opening.

Finish

45 With scissors, clip the corners and trim the edges of the outer seams.

46 At the opening, carefully pull the apron so that it is right-side out.

47 Push the corners out. Press.

48 Slipstitch the opening.

49 Topstitch ⅛" (3 mm) from the top of the apron and again at ⅝" (1.5 cm). 🍃

- - - - - - - - - - - - - - - - - - -

SARAH MINSHALL is a quilter, designer, and maker of all things fabric from Mason, Michigan. She has contributed to several books and has just begun her own line of patterns. Find out what she's up to next at her website, hiptopiecesquares.com.

Roll-Up Outdoor Concert Quilt

BY LISA CHIN

This quilt has two inside pockets to carry cups and a bottled beverage, as well as an outside pocket to carry the tickets, car keys, and a little cash. The top of the quilt is an easy pattern that showcases designer fabrics, while the back is made from durable, waterproof oilcloth. Once folded in half, the quilt can be rolled up and tied into an easy-to-carry "bag."

Materials

- [ ] 1 yd (91.5 cm) main cotton print fabric for the quilt top
- [ ] 1 yd (91.5 cm) secondary cotton print fabric for the quilt top
- [ ] 3/8 yd (34.5 cm) accent fabric (cotton print) for the handle and ties
- [ ] 48" × 60" (122 × 152.5 cm) piece of thin, lightweight batting
- [ ] Basting spray or safety pins
- [ ] Walking foot or a free-motion foot
- [ ] 1 yd (91.5 cm) of 1" (2.5 cm) wide webbing to strengthen the handle (for handle interior)
- [ ] 10" (25.5 cm) zipper
- [ ] Zipper foot
- [ ] 2 yd (183 cm) oilcloth for the quilt back
- [ ] Denim sewing machine needle

Finished Size

42" × 54" (106.5 × 137 cm)

✚ Sewing on Oilcloth - - -

Use a larger sized needle, such as a denim needle, and a longer stitch length when sewing on oilcloth. Sewing on the printed side of oilcloth can be a little sticky sometimes. Use a couple of your oilcloth scraps to determine which of the following tips works best for you and your machine:

+ Try a Teflon-coated presser foot, or stick a piece of masking tape to the bottom of your presser foot. A piece of masking tape on the oilcloth can work as well, but is sometimes difficult to remove completely.

+ Place a piece of tissue paper between your presser foot and the oilcloth. You can sew right through the paper and tear it off once finished.

Assemble the Quilt Top

1 Remove the selvedges from the main, secondary, and accent fabrics.

2 Cut a 20" (51 cm) × WOF (width of fabric) rectangle from the secondary fabric.

3 Using a 1/4" (6 mm) seam allowance, stitch the main and secondary fabrics together along the width of the fabric to create the quilt top.

4 Baste the quilt top to the batting using a basting spray or safety pins.

5 Using a walking foot or a free-motion foot, quilt through the top and batting.

6 Square up the quilted top.

The Inside Pocket

7 Cut a 15" × 16" (38 × 40.5 cm) rectangle from the secondary fabric to make the inside pocket.

8 Hem 1 of the shorter ends of the rectangle by folding the fabric under 1/2" (1.3 cm) and then again another 1/2" (1.3 cm). Press and topstitch the hem in place.

9 With the hem at the top, press the pocket under 1/2" (1.3 cm) along the left-hand side of the pocket rectangle.

10 Place the quilt top (right-side up) on a flat surface with the secondary fabric on the right. Place the hemmed pocket (right-side up) on the lower right corner, matching the raw edges with the raw edges of the quilt (**FIGURE 1**).

figure 1

11 Topstitch the folded left edge of the pocket to the quilt top, being sure to backstitch at the top of the pocket for extra security. Baste the remaining 2 edges of the pocket to the quilt top. (Leave the top of the pocket open.)

12 Measure 7" (18 cm) from the right-hand edge of the pocket at the top, middle, and bottom of the pocket. Connect the marks with a chalk line from the top to the bottom and topstitch along this line to form 2 pockets (**FIGURE 1**).

The Handle and Ties

13 From the accent fabric, cut one 2 3/4" (7 cm) × WOF strip and two 2 1/2" (6.5 cm) × WOF strips.

14 With right sides together, make each strip into a tube by sewing a 1/4" (6 mm) seam along the long edge of the strips. Turn the tubes right-side out and press flat. Insert the 1" (2.5 cm) webbing into the larger tube to form the handle. Cut the excess fabric from the length of the handle. Knot the ends of the ties to finish.

Tip

+ To avoid excess holes in your oilcloth, use binder clips, long paper clips, or clothespins to hold the oilcloth together while sewing.

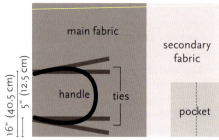

figure 2

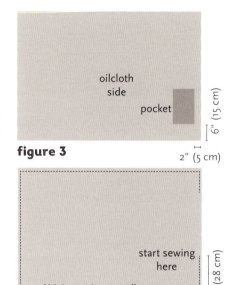

figure 3

figure 4

15 In preparation for securing the handle and ties to the quilt top, pin the raw edge of the handle 5" (12.5 cm) up from the lower left-hand corner and place the other end of the handle 16" (40.5 cm) up from the corner. Fold each tie in half and pin 1 to the inside of each side of the handle (**FIGURE 2**). Baste the handle and ties in place.

The Outside Pocket

16 Cut the oilcloth into a rectangle the same size as your quilt top (about 42" × 54" [106.5 × 137 cm]).

17 Cut 2 rectangles of oilcloth for the outside pocket: one 2" × 10" (5 × 25.5 cm) and one 6" × 10" (15 × 25.5 cm).

18 Place the raw edges of the long side of each rectangle along the zipper teeth and sew to the zipper using a zipper foot.

19 Place the pocket (right-side up) on the oilcloth (right-side up) by measuring 6" (15 cm) from the long edge and 2" (5 cm) from the shorter edge (**FIGURE 3**). Topstitch the pocket to the oilcloth backing. There is no need to turn under the edges of the pocket.

Assemble the Quilt

20 Place the quilt top on the oilcloth panel, right sides together, making sure that the oilcloth pocket and the ties are in the same corner (tuck the ties toward the interior).

21 Using a ½" (1.3 cm) seam allowance, start sewing about 11" (28 cm) from the first corner. Sew toward the first corner and continue around the edge of the quilt, leaving a 20" (51 cm) opening for turning (**FIGURE 4**). Clip the corners. Turn the quilt right-side out, push out the corners, and turn under the fabric at the opening. Starting at the turned-under opening, topstitch ¼" (6 mm) from the edge of the entire quilt.

22 Your quilt is now ready for you to insert a couple of plastic cups and a bottle of your favorite beverage into the two inside pockets. Fold the quilt in half lengthwise and roll it up toward the ties. Tie it up, put your tickets into the zippered pocket, and you are ready for your next outdoor concert. ✐

Visit LISA CHIN's blog at somethingcleveraboutnothing .blogspot.com.

Liberty & Linen Spring Hat

BY MELISSA FRANTZ

Welcome spring with a burst of Liberty floral print in this easy-to-make hat.

Materials

- ½ yd (46 cm) of linen or linen blend (at least 45" [114.5 cm] wide)
- ½ yd (46 cm) of cotton print (or a piece measuring at least 18" × 20" [45.5 × 51 cm]; shown here: Liberty floral print by Tana Lawn)
- ½ yd (27.5 cm) of flannel for brim lining (based on a 42" [106.5 cm] wide fabric)
- Pattern templates on page 15
- 24" (61 cm) of ½" (1.3 cm) wide twill tape
- Coordinating sewing thread
- Rotary cutter and self-healing mat
- Tailor's chalk or water-soluble fabric marker
- Pinking shears or serger

Notes

* All seam allowances are ½" (1.3 cm) unless otherwise noted.

* Outer Brim B and Inner Brim/Inner Brim Lining are all the same pattern piece. When cutting Outer Brim B, cut the whole pattern piece. When cutting the Inner Brim and Inner Brim Lining, fold the pattern piece under at the fold line, then place the fold line on the fold of the fabric.

Cut Out Fabric

1 Trace pattern pieces from the pattern insert on the wrong side of your fabric. Mark notches with chalk or fabric marker. Using a rotary cutter or scissors, cut out all pattern pieces as follows:

Cut 1 Outer Brim A on the bias (see Sewing Basics) from the linen or linen blend; Cut 1 Outer Brim Patch on the bias from the cotton print; Cut 1 Outer Brim B on the bias from the linen or linen blend; Cut 1 Inner Brim on a bias fold from the cotton print; Cut 1 Inner Brim Lining on a bias fold from the flannel; Cut 1 Side on fold from the linen or linen blend, notch at center front (directly on the fold line at the top of the pattern); Cut 1 Crown from the linen or linen blend.

Assemble Brim

2 Placing right sides together, pin Outer Brim A to Outer Brim Patch, matching up the notches. Sew together along the notched edge, then press the seam allowances open. Placing right sides together, pin Outer Brim B to the other side of the Outer Brim Patch, matching up the notches. Sew together along the notched edges and then press the seam allowances open. Fold this seamed piece in half widthwise with right sides together, matching up the short raw edges. Pin and then stitch together along the short edge; press the seam allowances open. You will now have the completed outer brim.

3 Placing wrong sides together, pin the Inner Brim and Inner Brim Lining pieces together, pinning along the long edges to hold in place. Fold the layered pieces in half widthwise with the right sides of the cotton print together, matching up the short raw edges. Pin and then stitch together along the short edge; press the seam allowances open. You will now have the completed inner brim.

4 Placing right sides together, pin the outer brim and inner brim pieces together (right side of linen to the cotton print), matching up the seams. Sew all the way around the bottom (wider) edge, trim the seam and clip the curve, then turn the completed brim right-side out and press flat with raw edges together.

Assemble Side and Attach Top

5 Fold the Side piece in half widthwise with right sides together, matching up the short raw edges. Pin and then sew together. Press the seam allowances to one side and pink, serge, or zigzag the seam allowances together.

6 Placing right sides together, match the notches on the Side piece to the notches on the Crown, pinning the raw edges together around the Crown. Carefully sew together, evenly distributing the fabric and easing as you go. Press the seam allowances to one side and finish as above.

Attach Brim and Sew in Hatband

7 Pin finished brim (from Step 4) to the free edge of the Side piece, with right sides together, matching up the raw edges and the back seams. Carefully pin together around the entire edge, evenly distributing the fabric. Sew together, easing as you go.

8 The twill tape acts as a hatband, covering the raw edges and adding more shape to the finished hat. With the hat inside out, start at the back seam and pin the twill tape to the seam allowance along the stitch line just made so that the twill tape lies on top of the seam allowances. Carefully stitch the twill tape down to the seam allowance only (make sure the rest of the hat is out of the way of the needle), stitching ⅛" (3 mm) inside the seam line. Press the twill tape/seam allowance toward the top of the hat. Trim the seam allowance as necessary so the raw edges are concealed by the twill tape.

9 Turn the hat right-side out and topstitch ¼" (6 mm) above the seam, around the hat, anchoring the twill tape and seam allowance in place.

10 Using tailor's chalk or a water-soluble fabric marker, draw three guidelines around the brim, starting ⅛" (3 mm) from the outer edge of the brim and at the center front of the hat. Draw the lines about ¾" (2 cm) apart in the front, gradually bringing them a little closer together toward the back. Topstitch the brim following the lines. 🍃

- -

MELISSA FRANTZ lives and sews in Portland, Oregon, with her partner and three boys. You can find her at allbuttonedup.typepad.com.

Enlarge all templates 200%

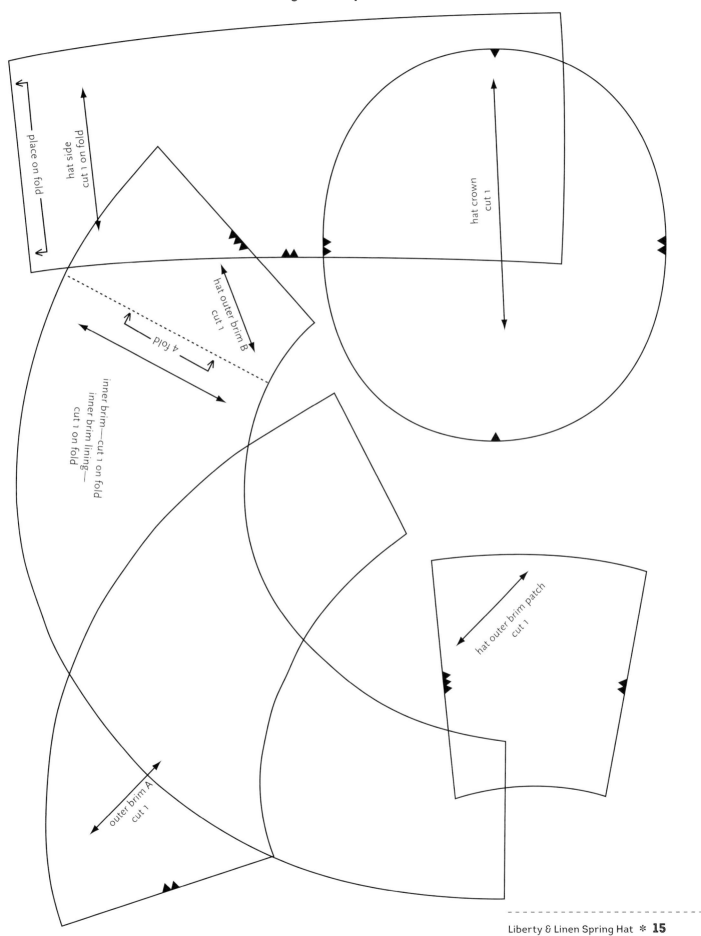

place on fold

hat side
cut 1 on fold

hat crown
cut 1

hat outer brim B
cut 1

4 fold

inner brim—cut 1 on fold
inner brim lining—
cut 1 on fold

hat outer brim patch
cut 1

outer brim A
cut 1

Water Bottle Carrier

BY DIANE RUSIN DORAN

When I go for a walk, I like to have my hands free. This cute water bottle sling is just the ticket for taking along some refreshment on a walk to admire beautiful spring flowers.

Materials

☐ Fabric scraps: 12 strips 1"–1½" × 8½" (2.5–3.8 × 21.5 cm)

☐ Solid fabric: 4" × 6½" (10 × 16.5 cm) rectangle for bottom; 2 strips 1½" × 21" (3.8 × 53.5 cm) for sides; 2" × 44" (5 × 112 cm) strip for strap

☐ Insul-Brite: 5½" × 21" (14 × 53.5 cm) rectangle

☐ Grosgrain ribbon, 2 pieces 2" (5 cm) long

☐ 2 D rings, ½" (1.3 cm) each

☐ Lining fabric: 5½" × 20¾" (14 × 52.5 cm) rectangle

☐ 2 lobster claw hooks, ½" (1.3 cm) each

Notes

✳ This carrier is sized to fit a half-liter water bottle.

✳ It is constructed as a long rectangle, on a foundation of needle-punched insulating material. The rectangle is folded in half to create the opening for the water bottle.

✳ I strip-pieced panels for the sides, and to avoid mismatched horizontal piecing, I chose to add a solid strip of fabric to the sides of my strip-pieced panels. If you desire, you can make your patchwork piece and the fabric for the bottom of the carrier wider and omit these long strips.

The Carrier

1 Strip-piece the 12 fabric scraps together to make an 8½" × 8½" (21.5 × 21.5 cm) square.

2 Cut the square in half perpendicular to the stripes so that you have 2 pieces 4¼" × 8½" (11 × 21.5 cm) with the stripes running horizontally.

3 Trim away a 1¼" × 3" (3.2 × 7.5 cm) rectangle from each side of the center of the Insul-Brite (this is to reduce bulk; **FIGURE 1**).

4 Center the 4" × 6½" (10 × 16.5 cm) solid fabric rectangle over the middle of the matte side of the Insul-Brite, and baste the short ends of the rectangle in place. This fabric will partially cover the trimmed-out area of the Insul-Brite (gray area in **FIGURE 2**).

5 With right sides together, sew 1 strip-pieced rectangle to each short end of the 4" × 6½" (10 × 16.5 cm) fabric rectangle. Flip the pieced area over, and baste the far end of each pieced section to the Insul-Brite.

6 Place a 1½" × 21" (3.8 × 53.5 cm) strip right-side down on each long side of the pieced unit, sew them in place, and flip the strips toward the outside edges.

7 Thread the D rings onto the 2" (5 cm) pieces of grosgrain ribbon and fold the ribbon pieces in half. Stitch through both thicknesses of ribbon close to the D rings. Center 1 piece of grosgrain on the right side of each end of the patchwork and baste the raw ends in place (**FIGURE 4**).

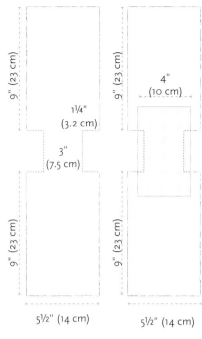

9" (23 cm) 1¼" (3.2 cm) 3" (7.5 cm) 9" (23 cm) 9" (23 cm) 4" (10 cm) 9" (23 cm) 5½" (14 cm) 5½" (14 cm)

figure 1   **figure 2**

figure 3

figure 4

Tip

+ If you already have an "orphan" quilt square, or even some fabric you really love, either can be substituted for this pieced area.

Tip

+ Make a light pencil mark 1" (2.5 cm) in from each long side of the Insul-Brite to help keep the long strips straight (**FIGURE 3**).

8 Fold the Insul-Brite-lined pieced section in half, wrong sides together, and firmly crease the fold. Unfold the piece and turn it wrong-side up. Measure 1½" (3.8 cm) on either side of the center fold. Crease on each mark across the width of the fabric, right sides together, creating 3 folds **(FIGURE 5)**. The folds will look like a "W" from the side. Pin the folds to hold them in position.

9 Repeat Step 8 with the lining fabric.

10 Put the lining on top of the patchwork piece, right sides together. Sew 1 short end of the lining to 1 short end of the patchwork piece. Press the seam allowance toward the lining and understitch the lining. *Note: The lining piece is slightly shorter than the outside piece to keep it rolled to the inside of the carrier when the project is complete.*

11 Repeat Step 10 for the other end of the patchwork piece. Cut the corners off of the seam allowance to reduce bulk.

12 Keeping the right sides together, realign the lining and the patchwork so that the 2 seams are on top of each other, with the right sides of the lining together and the right sides of the pieced area together. Be sure to keep the "W" folds in place, as they will create the flat bottom of the carrier **(FIGURE 6)**.

13 Sew the side seams, catching all folded areas in the seam and leaving 3"–4" (7.5–10 cm) open on the lining part of 1 seam. Press the seams open as much as possible, but do not apply the iron directly to the Insul-Brite.

14 Turn the carrier right-side out through the opening at the side, and slip-stitch the opening closed. Push the lining back down into the carrier.

The Strap

15 Press the 2" × 44" (5 × 112 cm) strip of fabric in half lengthwise, wrong sides together. Open up the fabric, and press the raw edges into the center fold. Press again.

16 On the short ends of the strip, turn the raw edges about ½" (1.3 cm) and press them in toward the center **(FIGURE 7)**.

17 Press the fabric strip in half again, with all of the raw edges enclosed, and topstitch the strap along all 4 edges.

18 Insert 1 end of the strap through 1 of the lobster claw hooks, fold the strap over about ½" (1.3 cm), and topstitch the end in place to attach it to the hook. Repeat for the other end of the strap. Attach the strap to the carrier by the lobster claw hooks.

19 Insert a water bottle into your carrier and go for a stroll! 🖋

Visit **DIANE DORAN'S** website at dianedoran.com.

figure 5

figure 6

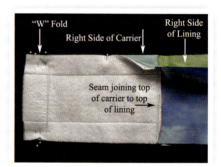

figure 7

Materials

- ☐ Cotton fabric scraps
- ☐ Coordinating fabric for underside
- ☐ Interfacing
- ☐ Thread
- ☐ Iron
- ☐ So Simple Headband template on page 20

So Simple Head Wrap

BY ELLEN SEEBURGER

This simple patchwork head wrap will add a burst of color to any outfit.

Make the Main Piece

Note: All seam allowances are ½" (1.3 cm) unless otherwise noted.

1 Select fabric scraps in varying widths and cut them in strips 8" (20.5 cm) long.

2 Piece the fabric so that you have a strip of fabric 8" (20.5 cm) long by 15" (38 cm) wide.

3 To create a patchwork effect, cut the strip in half resulting in 2 pieces, each 4" × 15" (10 × 38 cm). Take 1 piece and cut it into smaller strips. Once you have a pattern you like, sew the pieces together. The final piece of fabric should be 4" × 15" (10 × 38 cm).

4 Use the template and cut the pieced fabric, remembering to leave a ¼" (6 mm) seam allowance.

5 Use the template and cut the fabric for the underside, and a piece of interfacing.

6 Lay your pieced fabric right-side up, with the backing fabric right-side down on top, with the interfacing on top of the backing fabric. Sew the 3 pieces together, taking care not to sew the tapered ends closed. This is where the cords will need to be sewn later. In addition to leaving the tapered ends open, leave a 3" (7.5 cm) opening on 1 of the long sides.

7 Using the opening, turn the piece right-side out and press with a warm iron.

8 Make sure the tapered ends, where the cord will go through, are folded under, on the inside, and pressed.

Make the Cords

9 Cut 2 strips of fabric 3" × 10" (7.5 × 25.5 cm).

10 Lay the fabric facedown on your ironing board and fold over each edge lengthwise so that they meet in the middle of the fabric. Iron the edges down. The strip should now be 1½" (3.8 cm) wide.

11 Fold the strip in half lengthwise and iron.

12 Sew all the way around the edge of the fabric. Your cords are now ready to attach to the main piece.

Put It All Together

13 Insert the ends of the cords into the 2 tapered ends and pin.

14 Fold and iron the edges of the opening at the top and pin.

15 Sew all the way around the head wrap, with a ⅛" (3 mm) seam allowance, making sure that the cords are securely fastened.

16 Press with a warm iron. ✍

ELLEN SEEBURGER is the assistant editor of *Quilting Arts Magazine*. Visit her blog at quiltingdaily.com.

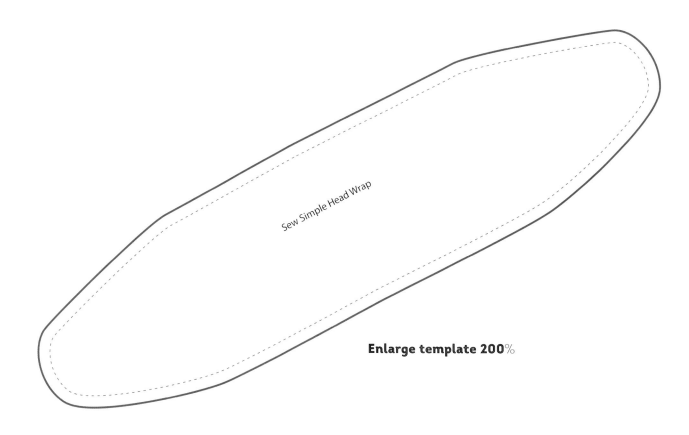

Sew Simple Head Wrap

Enlarge template 200%

Roll-Up Reversible Stadium Blanket

BY CAROL ZENTGRAF

No matter the weather, you'll be ready for game day with this reversible stadium blanket. Featuring cozy flannel on one side and water-resistant Supplex fabric on the reverse, it can be used to sit on or under. Clip-on straps with a handle make it easy to carry.

Materials

- 1⅝ yd (1.5 m) of 45" (114.5 cm) wide flannel fabric (Main; shown: green/brown plaid)

- 2 yd (1.8 m) of 60" (152.5 cm) wide water-resistant fabric, such as Supplex (Contrast; shown: brown)

- 44" × 54" (112 × 137 cm) rectangle of cotton batting

- Coordinating sewing thread

- Rotary cutter, rigid acrylic ruler, and self-healing mat

- Size 80/12 or 90/14 Microtex/sharp sewing machine needle

- 1¾ yd (1.6 m) of 1" (2.5 cm) wide nylon webbing

- Two 1" (2.5 cm) side-release buckles

Finished Size

44" × 54" (112 × 137 cm) flat (see Note)

Note

* If the flannel fabric is narrower than 44" (112 cm) after the selvedges are removed, alter the size of the other pieces to match the flannel.

Cut the Fabric

1 From the Main fabric, cut one 44" × 54" (112 × 137 cm) rectangle for the top of the blanket.

2 From the Contrast fabric, cut one 44" × 54" (112 × 137 cm) rectangle for the reverse side of the blanket. From the remaining fabric, cut 2¼" (5.5 cm) wide bias strips to total 210" (533 cm) for the binding.

Assemble the Blanket

3 Layer the Contrast piece (right-side down), the batting, and the Main fabric piece (right-side up), with the raw edges even. Make sure all layers are smooth, without tucks or stretched areas. Pin and then baste the edges of all layers together.

4 Sew the short edges of the binding strips together, using a ¼" (6 mm) seam allowance, and press the seams open. Press the strip in half lengthwise with wrong sides together.

5 Beginning near the center of one short edge, bind the quilt, referring to Binding with Mitered Corners, option B, (see Sewing Basics) and sewing the binding first to the Main fabric side of the blanket. When folding the binding to the reverse side of the blanket, bring the fold a scant ⅛" (3 mm) beyond the seam line. From the Main fabric side, stitch in the ditch, catching the binding fold in the stitching on the reverse side (rather than slip stitching).

6 Fold the blanket in half lengthwise (with Contrast fabric sides together) and roll into a compact bundle.

Make the Handle and Straps

7 From the nylon webbing, cut two 20" (51 cm) lengths for the straps and one 24" (61 cm) length for the handle.

8 Fold 2¼" (5.5 cm) to the wrong side on each end of the handle webbing and stitch the ends, sewing back and forth across the webbing and covering a 1" (2.5 cm) space below each raw end to secure.

9 Insert the 20" (51 cm) webbing lengths through the handle loops made in the previous step. Open the buckles and insert the webbing ends through the buckle openings, folding 1½" (3.8 cm) to the wrong side. Wrap the straps around the rolled-up blanket and adjust the strap lengths as desired, pinning the webbing ends in place.

10 Sew the strap ends as directed in Step 8.

11 Wrap the straps around the blanket and close the buckles. Slide the handle to the center of the straps to carry. 🍃

- -

CAROL ZENTGRAF is a writer, a designer, and an editor, who specializes in sewing, textiles, painting, and decorating. Her work has been published in several magazines and she is the author of several sewing books, including *Embellishments for Adventurous Sewing*.

Patchwork Lunch Sack

BY SARAH MINSHALL

Your lunch has never looked so pretty! The patchwork is quickly cut from a precut fabric bundle, and the sack is made with insulated batting to keep your meal at just the right temperature.

Materials

- ☐ Twenty-four 5" (12.5 cm) precut squares, cut in half to measure 2½" × 5" (6.5 × 12.5 cm), or 48 assorted quilting weight cotton scraps measuring 2½" × 5" (6 × 12.5 cm) (shown: prints in a variety of colors, patterns, and scales)

- ☐ ½ yd (46 cm) of coordinating cotton for Lining (shown: blue and green raindrop print)

- ☐ 22" (56 cm) of 1" (2.5 cm) wide cotton webbing for the handle (shown: white)

- ☐ 2½" (6.5 cm) of ⅝" (1.5 cm) wide Velcro (shown: white)

- ☐ ½ yd (46 cm) of Mylar/poly batting such as Insul-Bright

- ☐ 2¼ yd (2.06 m) of 2" (5 cm) wide coordinating premade bias tape (shown: white)

- ☐ Coordinating machine sewing thread (shown: white)

- ☐ Coordinating machine quilting thread (shown: white)

- ☐ Handsewing needle

- ☐ Rotary cutter, rigid acrylic ruler, and self-healing mat

- ☐ Curved (quilting) safety pins

- ☐ Walking foot for sewing machine

- ☐ Disappearing ink pen

Finished Size

8¼" long × 5¼" wide × 8¾" tall (21 × 13.5 × 22 cm)

Notes

* All seam allowances are ¼" (6 mm) unless otherwise noted.

* Press all patchwork seams to one side, alternating sides where the seams line up (to increase the accuracy of seam joins and corners), unless otherwise noted.

* Binding is sewn on by machine on one side only and is finished by hand using a slip stitch.

* It is very important that the sack pieces are sewn, cut, and trimmed accurately to ensure that the sack sits flat on the bottom and evenly on the sides. Follow the directions for squaring up the sack carefully.

* Test the fabric-marking pen on a scrap of fabric before you begin (follow the manufacturer's instructions) to make sure it will completely wash out.

Cut the Fabric

1 From the Mylar/poly batting (Insul-Bright), cut:

— One panel measuring 28" × 11" (71 × 28 cm); this piece will be called Batting

— Two pieces measuring 9" × 6½" (23 × 16.5 cm); these pieces will be called Batting Sides

2 From the Lining fabric, cut:

— One panel measuring 28" × 11" (71 × 28 cm); this piece will be called Lining

— Two pieces measuring 9" × 6½" (23 × 16.5cm); these pieces will be called Lining Sides

Sew the Patchwork

3 Determine the layout of the fabric for the patchwork. The long pieced panel of the sack includes the front, bottom, back, and top flap of the sack. Using the 2½" × 5" (6 × 12.5 cm) pieces, you will need to lay out six rows that are five rectangles wide each.

4 Working one row at a time, right to left in your pattern, sew (with right sides together) each rectangle to the next, following your layout design. Continue this until all six rows are pieced.

5 Press each row's seams flat to one side, alternating the direction from row to row so that the seams are pressed in opposite directions. Pin the rows together at the seam intersections.

6 Sew the rows together. The long panel is assembled; set aside.

7 For the two side panels, lay out three rows that are three rectangles wide each. Repeat Steps 5–7 to assemble the side panels; set aside.

Quilt the Panels

8 On a flat surface, layer the Lining right-side down, the Batting, and then the long panel, right-side up.

9 In preparation for quilting the Front Panel, pin-baste the three layers together, placing pins in the centers of the rectangular patches to hold the layers together. This keeps the pins out of the way when machine stitching the layers together.

10 In the same manner, pin-baste both Side panels.

11 Using a walking foot, machine-quilt the pinned panels by echo quilting ¼" (6 mm) away from the seams along all the seams. (Echo quilting refers to stitching multiple lines, equidistant from a design for emphasis.) Stitch on both sides of the seam lines of the rectangles.

Square Up and Round the Corners

12 Using a rotary cutter, rigid acrylic ruler, and self-healing mat, cut the Long panel to measure 8½" × 26½" (21.5 × 67 cm). Use the grid on the self-healing mat to line up your cuts to make sure the piece is as square as possible.

13 Using the same method, trim the two Side panels to measure 5¼" × 8½" (13 × 21½ cm).

14 With the Long panel right-side up and using a ruler, measure 2" (5 cm) in from each side of the corners of the short side that will be used as the flap, and make a small mark with a disappearing ink pen (**FIGURE 1**). Trace the edge of a saucer or other curved object to draw a curved line connecting each mark to make the rounded corners of the front flap. Using scissors, cut along the curved lines.

Assemble the Sack

15 Lay the long panel, right-side down, on a flat surface. With wrong sides together, lay one long edge of one side panel on top of the long panel, aligning sides, bottom edges, and outer corners **(FIGURE 2)**. Repeat with the second side panel, pinning both in place.

16 Sew along the edge of the sack, starting at the side top and stopping ¼" (6 mm) from the bottom edge of both side panels. Backtack to secure.

17 Fold the long panel, and pin it to the bottoms of the side panels. This will create the bottom of the sack.

18 Sew along one bottom side, starting and stopping ¼" (6 mm) from the corners. Backtack to secure **(FIGURE 2)**. Repeat for the second side.

19 Fold the remaining length of the long panel and pin it to the side panels. Sew the remaining side seams, starting at the bottom of the sack and stopping ¼" (6 cm) from the top of the side panel. Backtack to secure.

Sew the Bias Tape

20 Open the binding and pin it to the sack, with right sides together and raw edges even, starting at the front, right, outside corner of the top of the sack. Continue pinning down the right side, across the bottom side **(FIGURE 3)**, up the second side, over the front flap, down the left side across the side bottom, and ending at the top left corner. Sew the binding to the sack through all thicknesses, using a ¼" (6 mm) seam allowance. (This will be handsewn in place after the binding is sewn to the front edge).

21 With a new piece of binding, open the binding and pin it to the sack, with right sides together and raw edges even, starting at the front left corner. Sew across the side top, across the front edge, then across the right side ending at the back edge, sewing through all thicknesses.

22 Fold the binding over to the inside of the sack and pin all the way around the front and sides. Handstitch using a slip stitch.

23 Finish the remaining stitched binding by handstitching it around the sack's sides, bottom, and front flap using a slip stitch.

Finishing

24 Measure 22" (56 cm) of cotton webbing and fold over 1¼" (3.2 cm) at each end **(FIGURE 4)**. Pin it to one side panel 2¼" (5.5 cm) from the top, and centered from each side.

25 Begin sewing across the top of the handle ⅛" (3 mm) higher than the turned-in end of the folded-over cotton webbing, about 1⅜" (3.5 cm) from the bottom of the webbing **(FIGURE 4)**. Stop stitching ⅛" (3 mm) before the edge of the webbing, pivot at the corner, and continue stitching. Repeat for the remaining two sides, backtacking where the stitching began.

26 Repeat Steps 25–26 on the other side of the bag to attach the other end of the handle.

27 On the outside front of the sack, pin the hook side of the Velcro in place, measuring 2½" (6.4 cm) down from the front inside edge and centering it from the sides. Sew ¹⁄₁₆" (1.5 mm) from the edges around all sides and backtack at the end to secure.

28 On the inside of the front flap, measure 1½" (3.8 cm) up from the edge and, centering from the sides, pin the loop side of the Velcro in place. Sew ¹⁄₁₆" (1.5 mm) from the edges around all sides and backtack at the end to secure. ✎

- -

SARAH MINSHALL is a quilter, sewer, and maker of all things fabric related. Her giant heap of fabric keeps her busy in between life with her husband and pets in Michigan. She keeps tabs on what she makes at hiptopiecesquares.com.

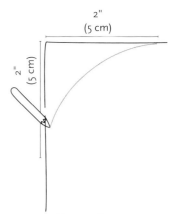

2" (5 cm)

2" (5 cm)

figure 1

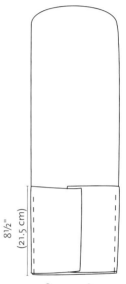

8½" (21.5 cm)

figure 2

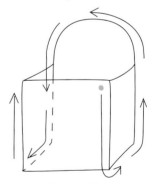

figure 3

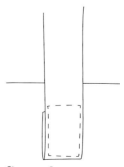

figure 4

Separating zippered sides make a quick change happen from tote to towel.

Convertible Beach Towel-Bag

BY ALI WINSTON

This oversize bag with nautical rope handles is perfect for the beach or pool. The tote is large enough to hold towels, toys, snacks, and lotions, while the outer pocket is the right size for your reading material. Settle in, unpack the bag, unzip the sides, and you have a towel for lounging. When you're ready to leave, simply zip up the sides and repack your tote.

Materials

- □ 1½ yd (137 cm) heavyweight fabric (such as Home Dec) for Exterior

- □ ½ yd (45.5 cm) coordinating cotton for Pocket

- □ ⅛ yd (11.5 cm) coordinating cotton solid for Handle Tabs

- □ 2 bath towels (standard size: 30" × 56" [76 × 142 cm])

- □ 6 yd (549 cm) clothesline

- □ 2 separating zippers, each 16" (40.5 cm)

- □ 1⅝ yd (148.5 cm) fusible fleece

- □ ½ yd (45.5 cm) single-sided fusible stabilizer, such as Peltex

- □ Zipper tab template on page 28

- □ Size 11 and 14 sewing needles

- □ Coordinating thread

- □ Zipper foot

Finished Size

Tote is 18" × 18" × 4" (45.5 × 45.5 × 10 cm) and opens to 18" × 54" (45.5 × 137 cm).

Notes

* Prewash towels to reduce the fuzz when they are cut, and to shrink them so the bag retains its shape when washed later. Prewash the fabric as well.

* Use towels that don't have a woven band at the ends to maximize the amount of usable terry cloth.

* Cut off the woven selvedges from the towels after you wash them. These edges shrink differently than terry cloth.

* Because towels have some stretch, try to stretch the towel slightly when cutting.

* Use fusible fleece and fusible stabilizer according to manufacturer's instructions

* Stabilizers are cut smaller than the exterior pieces to reduce bulk in the seams. Unless otherwise noted, center the pieces so that there is ½" (1.3 cm) of fabric on all sides.

* You will need a heavyweight (size 14) needle to sew through the rope and towel. A size 11 needle is recommended for sewing together the lighter-weight fabric pieces.

* Seam allowances are ½" (1.3 cm) unless otherwise noted.

Cut the Fabric

Main fabric (shown: aqua/green print):

— Cut 1 piece 19" × 41" (48.5 × 104 cm)

— Cut 1 piece 15" × 18" (38 × 45.5 cm)

— Cut 8 Zipper Tabs, each 2⅜" × 18" (6 × 45.5 cm)

Pocket fabric (shown: green print):

— Cut 2 Pockets 12" × 19" (30.5 × 48.5 cm)

Handle Tabs (shown: teal solid):

— Using Tab Template on page 28, cut 4 Handle Tabs on fold

Towel (shown: light blue):

— Cut 1 piece 19" × 41" (48.5 × 104 cm)

— Cut 1 piece 15" × 18" (38 × 45.5 cm)

Fusible stabilizer:

— Cut 1 piece 4" × 17¾" (10 × 45 cm)

— Cut 1 piece 11" × 17¾" (28 × 45 cm)

— Cut 4 Handle Tabs from template provided, cutting each on the fold

Fusible fleece:

— Cut two 18" × 18½" (45.5 × 47 cm)

— Cut one 14" × 17" (35.5 × 43 cm)

Handles:

— Cut six 36" (91.5 cm) pieces of clothesline

Make the Zipper Tabs

1 Divide the eight 2⅜" × 18" (6 × 45.5 cm) pieces into 4 pairs.

2 Separate the 2 zippers into 4 pieces.

3 Place 2 Zipper Tab pieces right sides together, sandwiching one "zipper half" between them. Place the bottom of the zipper ⅜" (1 cm) up from the bottom of the fabric. Attach the zipper foot. Sew through all 3 layers using a ¼" (6 mm) seam allowance.

4 To finish Zipper Tabs, sew ¼" (6 mm) from the top and bottom edges of the fabric. Clip corners and turn right side out.

5 Press the seams and topstitch tab sections.

6 Repeat Steps 4–6 with the other 3 Zipper Tabs.

Make the Handle Tabs

7 Apply fusible stabilizer to the wrong side of each of the 4 Handle Tabs.

8 On each Tab, fold down ¼" (6 mm) on the short edges. Then fold the Tabs in half, right sides together. Then sew down both sides using a ¼" (6 mm) seam allowance, making sure to sew

over the turned-down edges. Turn right-side out and press **(FIGURE 1)**.

Make the Handles

9 Place 3 pieces of rope together and sew 1" (2.5 cm) from the end, backstitching to secure.

10 Loosely braid the rope, ending and stitching 1" (2.5 cm) from the end to secure.

11 Repeat Steps 11 and 12 for the remaining Handle.

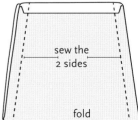

fold

sew the 2 sides

fold

figure 1

Make the Flap

12 Center the 14" × 17" (35.5 × 43 cm) piece of fusible fleece on the wrong side of the 15" × 18" (38 × 45.5 cm) piece of main fabric. Fuse.

13 Sew this piece to the 15" × 18" (38 × 45.5 cm) towel, right sides together, along three sides. Leave one of the long sides open for turning. Clip corners.

14 Turn the piece right-side out, press, and topstitch ¼" (6 mm) away from the three sewn sides.

Make the Pocket

15 Center the 11" × 17¾" (28 × 45 cm) piece of fusible stabilizer on one of the 12" × 19" (30.5 × 48.5 cm) pocket pieces. Fuse.

16 With right sides together, sew the fused piece to the other pocket piece along the long edges, leaving the sides open for turning.

17 Turn right-side out. Press. Topstitch ⅛" (3 mm) away from one long edge.

Assemble the Bag

18 On the wrong side of the 19" × 41" (48.5 × 104 cm) main fabric piece, measure 18½" (47 cm) from each short end (creating a 4" [10 cm] strip in the center). Center the 4" × 17¾" (10 × 45 cm) piece of fusible stabilizer on this strip and fuse.

19 For each 18" × 18½" (45.5 × 47 cm) fusible fleece piece, center the 18" (45.5 cm) side along the stabilizer edge and fuse.

20 For the placement of each Handle Tab, measure down 4" (10 cm) from top and sides on the right side of the Bag. Align the Tabs as shown **(FIGURE 2)**. Topstitch around the sides and the bottom, leaving the top open. Repeat for the other 3 Tabs.

21 Take a braided handle. Insert one end into the open end of the Handle Tab. Stitch in place along the top of the Tab, backstitching along the entire width to secure the handle. Attach the other end of this handle to the Tab on the same side. Repeat Step 22 for the other Handle.

22 On the outside of the 19" × 41" (48.5 × 104 cm) panel, measure down 18¼" (46.5 cm) from one short side, ¼" (6 mm) away from where the stabilizer starts. Line up the finished, but not topstitched edge of the pocket at this measurement. Topstitch ⅛" (3 mm) from bottom edge of pocket to secure in place **(FIGURE 3)**. Baste the sides of the pocket to the bag.

23 For zipper placement, mark a line 1" (2.5 cm) in from each long edge.

24 On the 1" (2.5 cm) mark, place 1 zipper piece (with the pull) right sides together aligning zipper tape with the raw edges of the bag. Baste zipper using a ¼" (6 mm) seam allowance.

25 On the long side, pin the other half of the zipper (without the pull), again aligning with the top of the fabric down 1" (2.5 cm) from the end. Baste in place.

26 Repeat Steps 24 and 25 with the other zipper flaps along the other long edge.

27 Pin the zipper flaps to the bag to keep them out of the way.

28 Align the center of the flap along the 19" (48.5 cm) side of the exterior on the side that does not have the pocket, right sides together. Baste in place ¼" (6 mm) from the edge. Pin down to keep it out of the way.

29 Take the 19" × 41" (48.5 × 104 cm) piece of towel. Lay it on top of the exterior with right sides together. Pin in place.

30 Using a ½" (1.3 cm) seam allowance, sew along all 4 sides, leaving a 10" (25.5 cm) opening along for turning along the 19" (48.5 cm) side without the flap. Zigzag or serge the raw edges.

31 Turn right-side out. Press the opening under ½" (1.3 cm).

32 Open out the flap. Topstitch ¼" (6 mm) around all sides of the main bag, making sure to sew across the handles, but not the extension or the zipper flaps. 🖋

- -

ALI WINSTON lives in Atlanta with her husband and hedgehog. She loves sewing and teaching math and combines the two on her blog asquaredw.com.

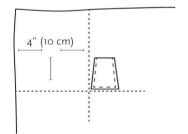

figure 2

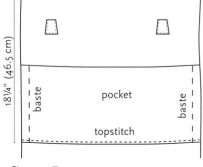

figure 3

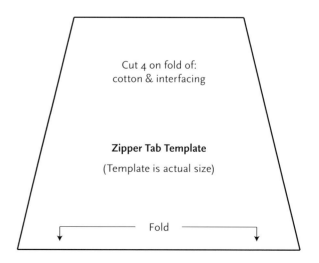

Cut 4 on fold of:
cotton & interfacing

Zipper Tab Template

(Template is actual size)

Fold

Quilt Sling

BY MARIJKA WALKER

Bundle your picnic quilt in this handy sling and you'll always be ready for fun!

Directions

1 For the fabric, roll your quilt as desired and measure the circumference, then subtract 5" (12.5 cm).

2 Cut 2 pieces of fabric 10" (25.5 cm) × the fabric measurement from Step 1. To prevent show-through, fuse interfacing to the back of 1 fabric.

3 With right sides together, sew ½" (1.3 cm) from each edge, reinforcing the corners, and leaving a 5" (12.5 cm) opening on 1 long edge. Trim the corners, turn the sling right-side out, and press, turning in the raw edges.

4 For the strap, multiply the fabric measurement from Step 1 by 2, and then add 47" (119.5 cm). Fold the strap in half and mark with a pin. Butt the ends together, ensure the webbing isn't twisted, and join with a wide zigzag.

5 Pin the webbing to 1 long edge of the sling, centering the butted ends. Ensure the webbing isn't twisted and pin the webbing to the other long edge, placing the pin at the center.

6 Sew around the entire sling and through the webbing, ¼" (6 mm) from the outside edge. Also sew ¼" (6 mm) from the inside edge of the webbing, pivoting to sew ¼" (6 mm) from the previous stitching on each short end.

7 Follow the manufacturer's instructions to attach heavy-duty snaps to the webbing, 3" (7.5 cm) from the sling. 🍃

- - - - - - - - - - - - - - - - - -

Visit MARIJKA WALKER's website at marijkawalker.com.

Lazy Days Hammock

BY CAROL ZENTGRAF

Swing the summer days away by chilling in this comfy reversible hammock. Easy to make with colorful print fabrics, the hammock also provides a stable and sturdy bed with its clever tab-and-dowel supports.

Materials

- □ 2½ yd (228.5 cm) each of two coordinating cotton prints for hammock (A and B)
- □ ⅔ yd (61 cm) of coordinating cotton print for tabs (C)
- □ 3½ yd (320 cm) of 45" wide (114.5 cm) fusible fleece
- □ 41" × 76" (104 × 193 cm) rectangle of low-loft batting
- □ 12 buttons, 1⅜" (3.5 cm) diameter
- □ ½" (1.3 cm) wide fusible web tape
- □ Two 1¼" (3.2 cm) diameter wood dowels, each 44" (112 cm) long
- □ Drill with ½" (1.3 cm) bit
- □ Two 2" (5 cm) diameter steel rings
- □ 13 yd (1.2 m) of ½" (1.3 cm) diameter polyester rope

Finished Size

43" × 82" (109 × 208.5 cm), not including tabs

Notes

* All seam allowances are ½" (1.3 cm).

* Sew seams with right sides together.

Cut the Fabric

1 For the top and reverse side center panels, cut one 43" × 63" (109 × 160 cm) rectangle from each hammock fabric (A and B).

2 For the contrasting borders, cut two 11" × 43" (28 × 109 cm) strips from Fabric A and Fabric B (4 borders total).

3 For the tabs, cut twelve 6" × 12" (15 × 30.5 cm) strips from C.

4 From the fusible fleece, cut two 43" × 81" (109 × 206 cm) rectangles and twelve 6" × 12" (15 × 30.5 cm) strips.

Construct the Hammock

5 To assemble the top and bottom panels, sew a contrasting border strip to each short side of the 43" × 63" (109 × 160 cm) center panel. Press the seams toward the borders.

6 Following the manufacturer's instructions, fuse the fleece to the wrong sides of both the top and bottom panels.

7 Layer the panels right sides together on a large flat surface. Then place the batting rectangle on top. Pin the layers together along all edges. Sew around all edges using a ½" (1.3 cm) seam allowance. Leave a 10" (25.5 cm) opening in one short edge for turning.

8 Trim the corners and turn the hammock right-side out. Press, tucking in the opening seam allowances. Slip-stitch the opening closed.

Decorative buttoned tabs work well to finish this hammock and hang it.

9 On one side of the hammock, use a chalk marker and long clear ruler to mark lengthwise stitching lines spaced 3" (7.5 cm) apart, beginning and ending at the border strips. *Note: If you are using a fabric with evenly spaced rows of motifs such as the featured geometric print, use the motif edges as a guideline instead of marking quilting lines.*

10 Pin the layers together across all marked lines. Stitch along the lines.

Make and Add Tabs

11 Fuse a fleece tab strip to the wrong side of each fabric tab strip.

12 For each tab, fold the strip in half with right sides together. Sew the long edges together, leaving a 2" (5 cm) opening in the center of the seam. Press the tab flat with the seam centered and the seam allowances open. Now stitch across each of the short ends. Trim the corners, turn right-side out, and press again. Slip-stitch the opening closed.

Choose large-scale tropical prints and let the fabric be the key design element.

13 On the seam side of each tab, fuse a strip of fusible web tape across each end and another strip across each end 2" (5 cm) from the first strip; do not remove the paper backing (**FIGURE 1**).

14 On one short end of the hammock, measure ¾" (2 cm) from a side edge and mark the placement on the top and underside. Remove the paper backing from the fusible web strips on one end of a tab and overlap the end of the hammock 2½" (6.5 cm), aligning the side edge with the ¾" (2 cm) mark (**FIGURE 2**). Fuse in place. Repeat for the opposite end of the same border. Repeat to position and adhere four more tabs between the two outer tabs, spacing them 5" (12.5 cm) apart. Fuse the remaining end of each tab to the bottom side of the hammock. Stitch the tabs in place.

15 Repeat Steps 13 and 14 for the opposite end of the hammock.

16 For both ends of the hammock, sew a button to each tab on both the top and the bottom of the hammock.

Prepare End Rods and Add Hammock

17 Drill a ½" (1.3 cm) diameter hole 1" (2.5 cm) from each end of both wood dowels. Make certain the holes are aligned. Slide the dowels through the tabs on each end of the hammock.

18 Wrap a piece of tape around each end of the rope to prevent raveling. Wrap a piece of tape around the center and cut the rope in half.

19 Use a double half-hitch knot to secure the center of each rope length onto a steel ring. Insert the rope ends through the holes in the dowels and knot securely. Remove the tape from the ends of the rope. If desired, seal the rope ends by carefully holding a lit match under the end—the heat will cause the polyester ends to fuse and prevent raveling.

20 Hang the hammock as desired on a hammock stand or between trees. 🍃

- -

CAROL ZENTGRAF is a writer, designer, and editor, specializing in sewing, embroidery, textiles, painting, and decorating. She designs for several magazines and fabric company websites. Carol is also the author of seven home decor sewing books.

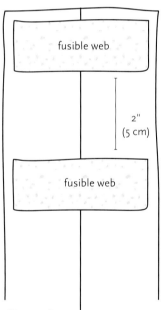

figure 1

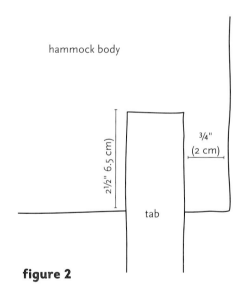

figure 2